The Fullness of the New Birth

Evangelism & Deliverance Manual

Nichol Collins

The Fullness of the New Birth

Copyright © 2020

GLOBE SHAKERS, LLC

This book or any parts thereof may not be reproduced in any form, or transmitted by any means; electronic, mechanical, photocopy, recording or otherwise is nor permitted without prior written permission of the author.

ISBN 978-1-965553-06-0

© 2020

Online store Covenant Gear @ Globeshakers.com

Email Globeshakers.com for Bulk orders of books at a discount (10 or more)

All rights reserved

Printed in the United States of America

Other Books

Amazon links on Website
https://globeshakers.com/pages/authors-corner
Behind Enemy Lines (autobiography)
I See Through Muddy Water (Signs of Down Low Men)
Power: The Benefits of Speaking in Tongues
Church Politics Vol. 1-4 The Mafia, Greed, Perverseness, Compromise
Under Construction: Men's LGBT Deliverance Manual
No Residue: Women's LGBT Deliverance Manual
Reaching the LGBT: Effective Evangelism
Walking in Power 30 Day Devotional
Attributes of Jesus 30 Day Devotional
The Seek 30 Day Devotional
Numerous Children's Books combating the LGBT agenda, abuse, and self esteem

Yevette Fisher's Books (My Mom)
Devil Let My Baby Go
Momma's Last Breath
What About Conrad
Holy Toledo
No One is Exempt
Walk by Faith Prayer Journal
In Between Trains

Table of Contents

Evangelism—The Heartbeat of God	1
The Path 2 Truth	11
Receive Power	40
Deliverance	46
Benefits of the Holy Spirit	74

Evangelism — The Heartbeat of God

Evangelism is not just a suggestion; it is the very heartbeat of God. From Genesis to Revelation, we see His relentless pursuit of mankind, calling us out of darkness into His marvelous light. As believers, we are His hands, His feet, and His mouthpieces in the earth. The Great Commission is not just for preachers or evangelists—it is for every born-again believer. The enemy would love nothing more than to silence us, to make us believe that sharing the gospel is optional or that we must have a certain personality to be effective. But the Word of God commands otherwise:

"But sanctify the Lord God in your hearts: and be ready always to give an answer to every man that asketh you a reason of the hope that is in you with meekness and fear." — 1 Peter 3:15

Everywhere we go—our workplaces, our families, the marketplace—we encounter souls who are searching, even if they do not realize it. They are searching for truth, for peace, for something that the world cannot offer. We, as the church, have

The Fullness of the New Birth

the answer. The gospel of Jesus Christ is the only hope for mankind, and we must never be ashamed to share it.

Paul, the great apostle and evangelist, warns us of the dangers of straying from the pure gospel: *"But though we, or an angel from heaven, preach any other gospel unto you than that which we have preached unto you, let him be accursed."*
— Galatians 1:8

This is why it is necessary to outline scripture as our foundation. The Word of God does not lie. It does not change based on opinions, denominations, or traditions. In these last and evil days, we cannot afford to be ineffective in our witness. We must set aside former indoctrinations, personal preferences, and any hesitation that keeps us from sharing the truth that saves.

We aren't witnessing a true move of the Holy Spirit because many are not prioritizing intimate time in prayer. The church must prepare for the harvest, which is plentiful, but the laborers are few (Matthew 9:37-38). Sadly, many have laid down the evangelism mantle, **captivated by** prophetic gifts, but the harvest of lost souls is the vital goal we must keep at the forefront.

The truth is, we all need Jesus. It's crucial not to view anyone's current situation as a "lost cause." Jude reminds us that some are won with compassion, while others are won with fear, hating even the garment spotted by the flesh (Jude 1:22-23). This reveals the deep responsibility we have to reach people, not only with truth but with love. Each of us plays a significant role in someone's life, and it's our job to make a positive impact, whether through a word of encouragement, sharing the gospel, or simply showing the love of Christ.

There were times in my own life when people spoke words that left an impression on me, even while I was living in sin. Those words were **seeds** planted in my heart that eventually led me to reconsider my choices. As believers, it's our responsibility to exhibit love and understanding, no matter where people are on their journey. We must not look down on others based on their walk of life, but instead, strive to connect with them by first understanding their experiences.

Because so many individuals have suffered trauma in various forms, we must approach them with sensitivity, practicing active listening and seeking to empathize with the challenges and discrimination they face. This is where true ministry begins—meeting people where they are.

The Fullness of the New Birth

Understanding their pain opens doors for the gospel to be received more fully.

At the core of it all is love. God's love is unconditional, sacrificial, and life-changing. When we allow that love to lead us, we can share the gospel in a way that truly resonates with the hearts of those we encounter. The fire of God is ignited and sustained through praying in the Spirit, which opens the heavens and allows God to pour wisdom into us, especially for ministry. The more time we spend with Him in prayer, the more equipped we become to reach others with power and purpose.

We live in a world desperate for hope—and this is a clear call to evangelism. The gospel is the power of God unto salvation (Romans 1:16), and we must never lose sight of that. Often, the power of God is revealed through simple acts: a shared testimony, a word of encouragement, or even just a moment of listening. Every interaction is an opportunity to plant a seed. It's not always about bringing someone to an immediate decision, but about giving them something to reflect on—something that leads them to Christ in His perfect timing.

As believers, we must remember: the harvest is plentiful, but the laborers are few. Are we truly being the hands and feet of Jesus? Are we reaching the lost, praying for a greater move of the Holy Spirit, and stepping into the gap with love and intentionality?

Evangelism is not just a task—it's a calling for every believer. It begins with empathy, love, and understanding. When we commit to spending time with God and align our hearts with His burden for the lost, we open the door to a mighty move of the Holy Spirit—one that transforms our lives and impacts the world around us.

If there was ever a time to be bold in our faith, it is now. The world is growing darker, deception is rampant, and souls are perishing daily without knowing Christ. We do not have the luxury of waiting for a "perfect moment" to evangelize. The Bible declares:

"Preach the word; be instant in season, out of season; reprove, rebuke, exhort with all longsuffering and doctrine." — 2 Timothy 4:2

The urgency of the gospel is real. The enemy understands this, which is why he fights so hard to keep believers silent. He tells us we are not qualified, that people do not want to hear us, that we might offend someone. But Jesus Himself said:

"Ye are the light of the world. A city that is set on an hill cannot be hid." — Matthew 5:14

The Fullness of the New Birth

If we are the light, how can we stay hidden? If we hold the truth, how can we withhold it from those who need it most?

Fear is one of the biggest barriers that prevents many believers from sharing the gospel. Whether it's the fear of rejection, not knowing what to say, or feeling inadequate, these fears are real but can be overcome through understanding our identity in Christ and the power of the Holy Spirit. In 2 Timothy 1:7, Paul reminds us, *"For God gave us a spirit not of fear but of power and love and self-control."* Overcoming fear begins with embracing the truth that fear does not come from God.

When we remember that evangelism isn't about us, but about God's power working through us, it helps shift our focus and remove the fear. Evangelism is not about having a perfect script—it is about being **led** by the Holy Spirit. Some of the greatest soul-winners were not eloquent speakers; they were simply **obedient.** Consider Moses, who tried to excuse himself from God's call because he was not a fluent speaker (Exodus 4:10). Yet God used him mightily.

For those who feel inadequate, remember this: the power is in the message, not the messenger. Paul himself admitted: *"And I, brethren, when I came to you, came not with excellency of speech or of wisdom, declaring unto you the testimony of God. For I determined not to know anything among you, save Jesus Christ, and him crucified."* — 1 Corinthians 2:1-2

God does not need us to be impressive; He just needs us to be **available.** Evangelism is not about building personal platforms, proving a point, or debating doctrine. It is about the lost coming to the saving knowledge of Jesus Christ. Paul urged the church:

*"Now I beseech you, brethren, by the name of our Lord Jesus Christ, that ye all speak the **same** thing, and that there be **no divisions** among you; but that ye be perfectly joined together in the same mind and in the same judgment."*
— 1 Corinthians 1:10

The enemy loves division because a divided church is a weak church. When we focus on non-essential differences rather than the gospel itself, we **hinder** the work of the kingdom. Souls are at stake, and our priority must be unity in truth.

Open-ended questions are a great way to initiate conversations about faith and guide someone toward the gospel. These questions create space for people to share their thoughts, beliefs, and

The Fullness of the New Birth

experiences, which opens the door for you to wisely introduce the truth of the gospel. Here are a few examples and how they can lead to meaningful discussions:

"Are you connected to a church?"

This question helps you understand if they are part of a faith community and can also open a discussion about the importance of church fellowship, spiritual growth, and how God uses the church to strengthen believers. You can then share your personal experience and invite them to explore church or ask about their church experience.

"What do you believe about God?"

Asking this question invites them to share their current views on God, which gives you insight into their understanding and beliefs. This can help you guide the conversation toward the gospel, clarify any misunderstandings, and explain who God is as revealed in Scripture.

"Have you ever received the Holy Spirit speaking in tongues?"

This is a more specific question that can lead into a conversation about the baptism of the Holy Spirit. You can explain how speaking in tongues is a sign of being filled with the Holy Spirit, emphasizing its role in empowering believers for effective living and evangelism. If they haven't experienced it, you could share how they can receive this gift.

"Do you believe that God has a plan for your life?"

This question taps into the idea of God's purpose and destiny for each individual. It can open the door to talk about God's love, His plans for good (Jeremiah 29:11), and how Jesus is the key to fulfilling that purpose. This can also lead to a conversation about salvation, the hope we have in Christ, and how God wants to work in their life.

A Charge to You: This is your time. This is your assignment. If you have ever felt hesitant, uncertain, or afraid, I challenge you to take the words in this book to heart. Souls are waiting. Heaven is rejoicing over each one that repents (Luke 15:7). Will you answer the call?

By the time you finish this book, you will be equipped, encouraged, and empowered to do what God has called all of us to do—proclaim the gospel of Jesus Christ with boldness. Sound doctrine is essential, and as believers, we must be grounded in the Scriptures, especially those centered around salvation. The Bible instructs us

The Fullness of the New Birth

to always be prepared to give an answer for the hope that is within us.

"But sanctify the Lord God in your hearts: and be ready always to give an answer to every man that asketh you a reason of the hope that is in you with meekness and fear." —1 Peter 3:15

This means we must have a **solid understanding** of God's Word, not only for our own faith but also to **effectively** share the gospel with others. In a **world full of deception**, many are led astray by **false teachings** and diluted versions of the gospel. Without a firm foundation in Scripture, we risk being unable to properly lead others to Christ.

Knowing these scriptures allows us to not only defend our faith but also guide others toward salvation with **clarity and truth**. Many are **seeking answers**, and as ambassadors of Christ, we must be prepared to give them—not with arrogance, but with humility, love, and wisdom.

The Path 2 Truth

"The acts of the flesh are obvious: sexual immorality, impurity, debauchery (sensuality), idolatry and witchcraft; hatred, discord, jealousy, fits of rage, selfish ambition, dissensions, factions, and envy; drunkenness, orgies and such like. I warn you, as I did before, that those who live like this will not inherit the Kingdom of God."
—Galatians 5:19-21 (NIV)

The flesh finds temporary satisfaction in sinful behavior, but in the long run, it leaves us **empty**. Our soul is on a spiritual quest, longing for true fulfillment. Once we grow weary of an unfruitful way of living, it will stir a desire for **change**. Regardless of past mistakes, if we follow **God's** Plan of Salvation, (not man's) we can receive forgiveness.

I was enjoying the pleasures of sin blinded by its consequences. As I walked away from the LGBT+ community in 2014, I adopted a saying: *I had to be OFF with people to be ON with God.* I was on a path of destruction, but thankfully, I

The Fullness of the New Birth

heeded the tugging on my heart. After time, I realized that some disconnections unlocked blessings that had been delayed due to distractions.

God's love for humanity is unexplainable. If anyone ends up in hell, it is by their **own choices** and actions, not by God's will. The Lord is not slack concerning His promise, as some count slackness, but is longsuffering toward us, not willing that **any should perish** but that all should come to repentance (2 Peter 3:9). To be saved and effectively overcome bondage we must adhere to the **scriptures**. If we are **obedient**, we will flourish. The Lord loves His creation so much and He does not want anyone to walk in the spirit of **error.** We can be in church for a lifetime and **not grasp the fullness** of the new birth. The scriptures are the best place to discover **vital truths.**

"Transformed" is defined as a thorough or dramatic change in form, appearance, or character. Jesus Christ completely turns lives around through the regeneration of the Holy Spirit. If biblical truths remain hidden, our efforts will be in vain. We can be sincere yet **still be wrong,** which is why God ensures we understand what He **requires to enter** the Kingdom of Heaven.

"Search the scriptures, for in them you think you have eternal life." —John 5:39

We cannot ignore God's Word or allow others to persuade us with **their own** philosophy or theology. Jesus Himself spoke about **water baptism and speaking in tongues** during His earthly ministry. We must not disregard anything that **Christ taught** or established. Mark 16:16-17 and John 3:1-7 are authoritative mandates given directly by Jesus.

*Jesus answered, "Verily, verily, I say unto thee, **Except** (unless) a man be born of **water** and of the **Spirit**, he **cannot** enter into the kingdom of God."* —John 3:5

Notice that Jesus repeats "verily" **twice** accentuating a **crucial point** we need to grasp. **If we only repent when is the water and Spirit implemented?** This passage should provoke us to obey the scriptures in its **entirety.** John 3:5 emphatically states the "water and Spirit" is **essential**. Look at the passage beginning from John 3:1-8. He refers to being born of the flesh (a natural birth), and born of the Spirit (a spiritual birth). In John 3:7-8, Jesus warns us not to be surprised, but **just do it!**

John 3:8 "The wind bloweth where it listeth, and thou HEARest the SOUND thereof, but canst not

The Fullness of the New Birth

tell whence it cometh, and whither it goeth: so is EVERY ONE that is born of the Spirit."

Verse Breakdown

"The wind bloweth where it listeth..."
The Greek word pneuma means both wind and spirit, symbolizing the Holy Spirit.
Jesus compares the movement of the Spirit to the wind: unpredictable, sovereign, and beyond human control or understanding.

"...and thou HEAR the SOUND thereof..."
You can't see the wind, but you HEAR it and feel its effects. Likewise, when someone is truly born of the Spirit, filled with the Holy Ghost, there will be AUDIBLE EVIDENCE.

On the Day of Pentecost, they ALL spoke in tongues, fulfilling Jesus' words in John 3 and establishing the sound of the new birth.

"...but canst not tell whence it cometh, and whither it goeth..." Just as you can't trace the exact path of the wind, the work of the Spirit is God-initiated and divinely orchestrated. It cannot be forced, manipulated, or manufactured by human effort.

"So is EVERY ONE that is born of the Spirit."
Everyone truly born of the Spirit experiences

clear, "undeniable evidence." The Spirit's presence is not just felt; it's HEARD.

Just as the blowing wind cannot be ignored, a GENUINE Holy Ghost baptism is undeniable and unmistakable. The "sound" Jesus mentions isn't symbolic, it's LITERAL and audible. This verse affirms the biblical pattern of speaking in tongues as the **initial evidence** of receiving the Holy Ghost (Acts 2:4). Being born of the Spirit is NOT a quiet, inner-only transformation. It is a supernatural encounter that marks the believer with POWER.

Acts 8:12–18 further confirms this truth:
The Samaritans believed and were baptized in Jesus' name by Philip, yet NONE received the Holy Ghost until Peter and John came to lay hands and pray. This shows there is more to the new birth than belief alone, there must be a Spirit-filled encounter.

Repentance is the starting point, not the finish line.

*Jesus said, "He that **believeth** and is **baptized** shall be (future tense) saved: but he that believeth not shall be damned. And these signs shall follow them that believe; In my name shall they cast out Devils; they shall **speak with new tongues**." —Mark 16:16-17*

The Fullness of the New Birth

Jesus reaffirmed the necessity of the water and Spirit new birth documented in the Great Commission in Mark. Then, in **Matthew 16** he inquired about the rumors circulating about him. The disciples elaborated that some assumed that maybe he was John the Baptist, Elijah, Jeremiah or one of the prophets. Specifically, Peter was personally asked for his opinion of Jesus' identity. He replied, ***"You are the Christ, the Son of the living God."*** Jesus knew instantly that was not revealed by human knowledge.

"And I will give you the keys of the Kingdom of Heaven. Whatever you forbid on earth will be forbidden in heaven, and whatever you permit on earth will be permitted in heaven."
—Matthew 16:19 (NLT)

The ***"keys of the kingdom of heaven"*** are only mentioned ***once*** in the Bible. They were **given to Peter**. Jesus delegated him with the badge of authority. On the Day of Pentecost, Peter used those **spiritual keys** to proclaim the **Plan of Salvation** in Acts 2:38. The **first altar call** in Acts 2:37 they asked, **"What must we do?"**

As a reference point, turn to Acts 1:3-9. As we can see, Jesus spent 40 days after His resurrection giving instructions to his disciples (followers). He also mentioned John baptized with **water** but the **Holy Spirit** would be poured out in a few days (Acts 1:5). Jesus reiterated the **water and Spirit again.** His final words to conclude his earthly ministry were, **"Wait for the promise."**

*"But ye shall receive **power after** that the Holy Ghost is come upon you: and you shall be my witnesses."* —Acts 1:8

We cannot live holy without the Holy Spirit.

Satan tries to convince believers that speaking in tongues isn't for everyone—but that's a lie meant to keep us from walking in spiritual authority and advancing in rank.

We can't win spiritual battles without being properly equipped. The Holy Ghost—with the evidence of speaking in tongues—is part of the full armor God has made **available** to us. As believers, we should desire everything God has promised—not just settle for **partial** truth. Don't just talk about power—receive it, walk in it, and let it flow through you.

Now, let's summarize this chain of events in Acts chapter two. Read Acts 2:1-4 and notice, they ALL were filled and spoke in other *tongues*. Browse down to **Acts 2:13-17** and see how critics began to accuse them of being drunk on new wine. Peter stood up to address the crowd

The Fullness of the New Birth

because **remember** he was delegated with the *"Keys of the Kingdom."* Peter declared in Acts 2:17 that the outpour of the Holy Spirit is a **fulfillment** of what was foretold by the Prophet Joel. God said, *"I am pouring out my Spirit upon **ALL flesh** in the last days"* (Joel 2:28, Acts 2:17). Peter proceeded to preach a sermon. He began to remind the onlookers of all the miracles they witnessed Jesus perform (Acts 2:22-24), but yet they crucified him anyway. Peter testified that he and the others with him were eyewitnesses to Jesus' resurrection (Acts 2:32).

The 1st Century Altar Call

*"Now when they heard this, they were pricked in their heart, and said unto Peter and to the rest of the apostles, Men and brethren, what shall we do?" Then Peter said unto them, "**Repent**, and **be baptized every one** of you in the **name of Jesus Christ** for the remission of sins, and ye shall **receive** the **gift** of the **Holy Ghost**. For the **promise** is unto you, and to your children, and to all that are afar off, even as many as the Lord our God shall call. And with many other words did he testify and exhort, saying, **Save yourselves** from this untoward generation."* —Acts 2:37-40

There is no period after the word "repent" in Acts 2:38; the comma indicates a **continuation**. The rest of the verse states that everyone should be baptized in the **name** of Jesus Christ **and** receive the gift of the Holy Spirit. When baking a cake, all the ingredients <u>must be added</u> for a successful recipe. Similarly, we <u>cannot leave out steps</u> of salvation and <u>assume</u> we are saved. The Lord loves us so much that if we are truly **sincere**, He guides us to the **truth**. It is our choice to humbly obey the Word of God.

The Bible NEVER said that baptism was an outward expression of an inward work, a symbolic ritual, or public display to proclaim your belief.

Exodus 12:7 serves as a powerful **type and shadow** of salvation, illustrating the **threefold** plan of redemption. In biblical terms, a *type and shadow* is an Old Testament event, practice, or symbol that foreshadows a greater spiritual reality revealed in the New Testament. In this case, the Israelites were **required** to apply the blood of the Passover lamb to **three sides** of the doorpost—both side posts and the upper post. This was not a *random* ritual but a divine instruction that ensured their protection. **Partial obedience** would have resulted in death; if they had only applied the blood to "one" side, their firstborn would have perished.

This foreshadowed the New Testament plan of salvation, revealed in **Acts 2:38**, which also

The Fullness of the New Birth

carries a **threefold** requirement for escaping eternal judgment. Just as the Israelites had to fully obey God's instructions to be spared from death, we too must fully obey the gospel. **Salvation is not a partial experience**—it requires faith and obedience to God's complete plan. Here's how each step of *Acts 2:38*—Repentance, Baptism in Jesus' Name, and Receiving the Holy Ghost—is reflected in Old Testament *types and shadows*:

1. Repentance → Israel's Exodus from Egypt

In Exodus, the Israelites were enslaved in Egypt, representing **sin and bondage**. When God sent Moses to deliver them, they had to **choose to leave Egypt behind**, symbolizing repentance. *Repentance* is the first step in salvation because it means turning away from sin and surrendering to God. Just as the Israelites could not remain in Egypt and expect deliverance, we cannot continue in sin and expect salvation.

2. Baptism in Jesus' Name → The Crossing of the Red Sea

After leaving Egypt, the Israelites faced the Red Sea. When they passed through the water, **Pharaoh's army (symbolizing their past bondage) was buried and destroyed** (Exodus 14:26-28). This event foreshadows **baptism in**

Jesus' name, where our sins are washed away and buried (Acts 22:16). The Apostle Paul confirmed this in **1 Corinthians 10:1-2**, saying that the Israelites were *"baptized into Moses in the cloud and in the sea."* Likewise, we are baptized into Christ, taking on His name and receiving His righteousness (Galatians 3:27).

3. Receiving the Holy Ghost → The Cloud and Fire Leading Israel

After crossing the Red Sea, the Israelites were led by **a pillar of cloud by day and a pillar of fire by night** (Exodus 13:21-22). This represents the Holy Spirit, which guides and empowers believers. In the New Testament, **the Holy Ghost is the fire from heaven that fills believers** (Acts 2:3-4). Just as the cloud and fire signified God's presence among Israel, the Holy Spirit today marks believers as God's own and equips them for the journey of faith.

The Complete Pattern: Passover, Red Sea, and God's Presence

1. Blood on the Doorposts (Passover) → Jesus' Blood Applied in Repentance
2. Passing Through the Red Sea → Baptism in Jesus' Name
3. The Cloud and Fire Leading Them → The Holy Ghost Filling Believers

The Fullness of the New Birth

Salvation is a complete process, not a single event. Just as Israel had to follow **all three** steps to reach the Promised Land, we must fully obey Acts 2:38 to enter the Kingdom of God.

Some may dispute this by pointing to the **Thief on the Cross** beside Jesus, arguing that baptism and receiving the Holy Spirit are not required. This assumption is false, as the Crucifixion took place during the dispensation (era) of the **Law.** Jesus had **not yet** ascended into heaven (Acts 1:9) nor sent the gift of the Holy Spirit (Acts 2:1-4). The event described in Acts 2 marks the shift in time that placed us under GRACE on the Day of Pentecost, when the New Testament church was established. While salvation is a finished work of the cross, it **must** be appropriated by **obeying Acts 2:38**. Faith is not merely belief; it is **an action** that requires a **response**.

Jesus said, *"No man can come to me, except the Father which hath sent me draw him"* (John 6:44). There must be within, a sincere desire to completely change. The Greek word for repentance is *metanoia*, which means to change one's mind.

Water baptism is a cleansing process that requires **faith** in the shed blood of Jesus, which grants us forgiveness and remission of sins.

Peter also tells us that *baptism also* **saves us** *and is an answer of a good conscience toward God* (1 Peter 3:20-21). The primary purpose of baptism is to **demonstrate** your faith in a crucified, buried, and risen Savior. It is an act of **obedience** and a transliteration of the Greek word *Baptizo*, meaning to immerse.

Our Savior Jesus was without sin, but he was baptized to fulfill all righteousness, so we know we need to do it!

I love sharing this testimony about my mom. As a child, her grandfather—a Methodist pastor—sprinkled her with water in the titles of the Father, Son, and Holy Ghost. At age 24, she was baptized again by full immersion, but still "in the titles."

In the years that followed, several strangers crossed her path, each one telling her, "God wants to save you." She grew frustrated, believing she was already saved simply because she had confessed Christ as her Savior.

At 28, everything changed. A former co-worker—once a devout Jehovah's Witness—had experienced a life-changing encounter: she'd been baptized in Jesus' name and filled with the Holy Spirit. She invited Mom to visit her new Apostolic-Pentecostal church.

The Fullness of the New Birth

At the end of the service, something unexpected happened. Mom felt herself being *pushed* down the aisle. Thinking her co-worker was behind her, she turned to say, "Get your hands off me!"—but no one was there. The woman was still seated.

That's when she realized: **the invisible hand of God** was guiding her to the altar. As she walked, she heard a whisper in her spirit:
"Eternity is too long to be wrong."

In that moment, she didn't hesitate. She was ready to run and dive into the baptismal pool. She was baptized in the name of **Jesus Christ**, and this time—she knew it was different. Mom felt spiritually cleansed and deeply assured that this was true obedience to the Word of God—not tradition, not assumption, but truth.

That phrase—**"Eternity is too long to be wrong"**—was no longer just a whisper. It became a **life-altering conviction** that she could no longer ignore.

*"Or don't you know that all of us who were baptized into **Christ Jesus** were baptized into His death? We were therefore buried with Him through baptism into death in order that, just as Christ was raised from the dead through the glory of the Father, we too may live a new life."*
—Romans 6:3-4 (NIV)

"As far as the east is from the west, so far has He removed our transgressions from us."
—Psalm 103:12

*"When they heard this, they were **baptized** in the name of the Lord **Jesus**."* —Acts 19:5

*"And now what are you waiting for? Get up, be **baptized** and wash your sins away, calling on His **name**."* —Acts 22:16 (NIV)

"For as many of you as were baptized into Christ have put on Christ."
—Galatians 3:27 (ESV)

*"Thou believest that there is **one** God; thou doest well: the Devils also believe, and tremble."*
—James 2:19

*"Now when the apostles which were at Jerusalem heard that Samaria had received the word of God, they sent unto them Peter and John: Who, when they were come down, prayed for them, that they might receive the Holy Ghost: (For as yet he was fallen upon none of them: only they were **baptized** in the **name** of the **Lord Jesus**)."* —Acts 8:14-16

Matthew 28:19 is one of the most **misunderstood** verses in the Bible. It was not a baptismal event, but rather as a **responsibility** to

The Fullness of the New Birth

be fulfilled. "Go ye therefore, and teach all nations, baptizing them in the name of the Father, and of the Son, and of the Holy Ghost." The word "nations" is plural, clearly indicating the call to evangelize globally. "Baptizing them" refers to all genders, age groups, and ethnicities (plural). The command was to baptize "in the NAME," which is singular. Jesus' instructions were not to use the titles of Father, Son, and Holy Spirit as a formula for baptism.

*"And whatsoever ye do in word or deed, do **all** in the name of the Lord **Jesus**, giving thanks to God and the Father by him."* —Colossians 3:17

Should we exclude baptism? ^^^

We pray over our food in the name of **JESUS**, demons are cast out in the name of **JESUS**, and we lay hands on the sick by faith to be healed in the name of **JESUS**. Satan knows that the **power is in the name of JESUS**, so he will even allow someone to be baptized using the **titles** "Father, Son, and Holy Spirit," which fail to implement the **name** of JESUS. When Jesus was baptized, He Himself authorized and commissioned it. John the Baptist acted under His direct authority, making Jesus' baptism performed in His own name.

For by grace are ye saved through faith; and that not of yourselves: it is the gift of God: not of works, lest any man should boast (Ephesians 2:8-9). This passage in Ephesians is referring to works as the LAW specifically talking about the Israelites. Baptism is not a work, but rather a **command.** Paul was contrasting between GRACE and the LAW and in Verses 12-15, which by the works of the law no flesh shall be justified (Gal. 3:10, Deut. 27:26, Rom. 11:5). The water and Spirit new birth is the path we all should take.

We, as human beings, are made up of a body, soul, and spirit, yet we are **ONE** person identified by our name. There is NO baptism in the entire Bible performed using the "titles" of the Father, Son, and Holy Ghost. The Britannica, Canney, and Hastings encyclopedias have recorded that the early church **always** baptized in the **name** of the Lord Jesus until the development of the Trinity doctrine. The Roman Catholics shifted to sprinkling babies and adults, moving away from the practice of immersion.

"Hear, O Israel: The Lord our God is ONE Lord" (Deut. 6:4) cannot be contradicted. The NAME has caused controversy for centuries, and even King Herod tried to kill baby JESUS. The twelve apostles NEVER subscribed to the Trinity. In fact,

The Fullness of the New Birth

they were commanded not to "speak or teach" in the NAME of JESUS (Acts 4:18 NLT).

The Trinity doctrine was introduced under pressure from political circles, aiming to establish a consensus. It was enforced by the Byzantine Empire, dictating what all Christian churches were to believe—whether they "liked it or not!" The worship of triads or groups of three gods had been common in ancient cultures, such as Babylonia, Egypt, Greece, and Rome, long before, during, and after Christ. After the death of the Apostles, these pagan beliefs began to infiltrate Christianity. The philosophies of Plato, who lived about 400 years before Christ, paved the way for these ideas, with his teachings on the Trinity influencing the development of black magic, geometry, and religion.

"There is no other name under heaven given among men whereby we can be saved."
—Acts 4:12

Jesus is the "one name" for all three titles. He made it clear that 'repentance and remission of sins' should be preached in **His name**, beginning at Jerusalem, as stated in Luke 24:45-49. This passage also outlines the Great Commission. The historic event at Pentecost took place in Jerusalem, where Peter boldly declared that everyone should be baptized in the **name** of Jesus Christ for the **remission of their sins.**

*Jesus said, "I am come in my **Father's** name."*
—John 5:43

Jesus said, *"Me and my **Father** are **ONE**."*
—John 10:30

Jesus answered: *"Don't you know me, Philip, even after I have been among you such a long time? Anyone who has seen me has seen the **Father**. How can you say, 'Show us the Father?"*
—John 14:9 (NIV)

*"She will give birth to a **son**, and you are to give him the name Jesus, because he will save his people from their sins."* —Matthew 1:21 (NIV)

*"But the Helper, the **Holy Spirit**, whom the Father will send in My name, He will teach you all things, and bring to your remembrance all things that I said to you."* —John 14:26 (NKJV)

God is the Father in creation, the Son in redemption, and the Holy Spirit who dwells inside of us. Jesus is the **saving name** (Col. 3:17, Acts 4:12). Peter **confirmed** in Acts 2:38 what was stated in Matthew 28:19. All throughout the book of Acts baptism was **ONLY** performed in the **name** of the Lord **Jesus Christ.**

The Fullness of the New Birth

"That if thou shalt confess with thy mouth the Lord Jesus, and shalt believe in thine heart that God hath raised him from the dead, thou shalt be saved." —Romans 10:9

Several people are misled into believing that Romans 10:9 tells them how to "get saved." However, Romans 1:7 clearly states that this letter is written to **the saints** in Rome. In the original Greek translation, the word for "confess" is *Homologeo*, which means: not to deny, to say the same thing as another (as in being repetitive in your confession). The word "saved" in Romans 10:9 comes from the Greek word *Sozo*, which means to make safe or rescued (secure in God). The Greek word for salvation, *Soteria*, is <u>not used</u> in this passage to define "saved."

While confession and belief are gateways, Scripture emphasizes the ENTIRE new birth experience. Romans 10:9 urged that faith in the resurrected Christ and a willing confession of His Lordship are vital spiritual MAINTENANCE, that was NOT an altar call. Pentecost was before the writing of this letter. FULL obedience to the gospel includes repentance, baptism in Jesus' name, and the infilling of the Holy Spirit, as seen throughout the book of Acts. The book of Acts gives the complete picture of what it means to be born again (John 3:5).

Paul's concern for Israel was to forsake the law of Moses as a prerequisite for salvation and to focus on the new covenant through Jesus Christ. Chapters 9, 10, and 11 of Romans are addressed to the Jews, whom God chose for a task traced back to Abraham in Genesis. Later, the Jews rebelled and rejected Jesus as the Messiah. Thus, the context of these letters in Romans 9, 10, and 11 signifies that only a remnant of Jews would be saved. John 9:22 says, *"The Jews already agreed that anyone who confessed Christ would be thrown out of the synagogue."* Despite the backlash, Israel is being admonished in Romans 10:9 to keep believing, stay the course (Acts 2:42), and avoid being deterred by every kind of false doctrine (Ephesians 4:14).

We cannot build a doctrine from one verse!

WE MUST BE BORN AGAIN OF WATER & SPIRIT

*"They were **all** filled with the Holy Ghost, and began to speak with other **tongues**, as the Spirit gave them utterance."* —Acts 2:4

The terms *Holy Ghost* and *Holy Spirit* mean exactly the same thing. The phrase Holy Ghost is simply an older term that is predominantly used in the King James Version. Considering the word *ghost* has a different meaning today than it did

The Fullness of the New Birth

back then, modern translations of the Bible always use the Holy Spirit.

The Holy Spirit is our divine ability to take authority over demonic principalities. Without being filled with God's Spirit, having only earnest intentions to walk with God will not stand against the pitfalls, persecution, and relentless seduction from the enemy. We need strategic tools to deal with such a cunning adversary. Satan cannot interpret when a Believer speaks in tongues, which is why he tries to make people believe they do not need it.

*"And it shall come to pass in the last days, saith God I will pour out my Spirit upon **all flesh**: and your sons and daughters shall prophesy, and your young men shall see visions, and your old men shall dream dreams."* —Acts 2:17

There was a God-fearing man named Cornelius who gave food and money to the poor in Acts chapter ten. The Lord sent angels to both Peter and Cornelius in a vision, giving them instructions on how to meet each other. Despite his good deeds, Cornelius still needed to be saved. Peter preached the good news to Cornelius, his family, and friends.

"While Peter spake these words, the Holy Ghost fell on all them which heard the word. And they of

*the circumcision (Jews) which believed were astonished, as many as came with Peter, because that on the Gentiles (non-Jews) also was poured out the **gift of the Holy Ghost**. For they heard them speak with **tongues**, and magnify God. Then answered Peter, Can any man forbid water, that these should not be baptized that received the Holy Ghost as well as we? And he commanded them to be **baptized** in the <u>name</u> of the **Lord**."* —Acts 10:44-48

Receiving the Holy Ghost first did not make Cornelius and his household exempt from baptism. Remember, in John 3:5, Jesus said, "You must be born again of water and of Spirit, or you cannot enter the kingdom of God." When the Holy Spirit comes in, tongues (a heavenly language) will flow out. John 3:8 references, "When the Spirit comes, you will hear the sound thereof." God wants everyone to be filled with the Holy Spirit, and it is being poured out on ALL flesh (Joel 2:28, Acts 2:17).

*"When they heard this, they were **baptized** in the <u>name </u>of the Lord **Jesus**. And when Paul had laid his hands upon them, the Holy Ghost came on them; and they spake with **tongues**, and prophesied."* —Acts 19:5-6

Acts 19:1–6 – Disciples of John the Baptist

The Fullness of the New Birth

Paul finds believers who had only received John's baptism. He baptizes them in Jesus' name, then lays hands on them and they receive the Holy Ghost, speaking in tongues.

To utilize any of the "9 gifts of the Spirit" found in 1 Corinthians 12:1-11, we need the baptism of the Holy Spirit with the initial evidence of speaking with other tongues. Some mistakenly confuse one of the 9 spiritual gifts, called "divers kinds of tongues," with the infilling of the Holy Spirit. The operation of that particular gift occurs when a believer speaks in several languages.

When you speak in tongues for the first time, it is an encounter that leaves you speechless. No one will be able to persuade you that God does not exist. It is a miracle to speak in a language you were never taught. Every burden you carry is released through your prayer language unto the Lord.

The New Testament Plan of Salvation, from the Day of Pentecost until Jesus returns, is found only in Acts 2:38. The gospel spread thereafter, and other ministries were established. Consistent biblical documentation of water baptism in the name of Jesus Christ and speaking in tongues can be found.

In the New Testament, from Romans to Jude, the letters are written to saints—those who are **already saved**. As a whole, the Epistles tend to address three general issues: doctrine, application, and logistics. By reading the Epistles, we can learn how to **maintain** our salvation, **operate** in our gifts, **safeguard** order in the church, and look forward to Christ's return, among other teachings. However, we cannot reference these letters (Romans to Jude) as a means of leading the unsaved to the Lord, as they are directed to those already part of the faith.

Introductory Greetings to Local Churches

- Rom. 1:7: To all that be in Rome, beloved of God, called to be saints.
- 1 Cor. 1:2: Unto the church of God which is at Corinth, to them that are sanctified in Christ Jesus, called to be saints.
- 2 Cor. 1:1: To the church of God which is at Corinth, with all the saints who are in all Achaia.
- Gal. 1:2: To the churches of Galatia.
- Eph. 1:1: To the saints who are in Ephesus, and faithful in Christ Jesus.
- Phil. 1:1: To all the saints in Christ Jesus who are in Philippi, with the bishops and deacons.

The Fullness of the New Birth

- Col. 1:2: To the saints and faithful brethren in Christ who are in Colosse.
- 1 Thess. 1:1-2, 2 Thess. 1:1: To the church of the Thessalonians.
- 1 Tim. 1:2, 2 Tim. 1:2: To Timothy, a true son in the faith... a beloved son.
- Titus 1:4: To Titus, a true son in our common faith.
- Philemon 1:1: To Philemon, our beloved friend and fellow laborer.
- Heb. 1:2: Has in these last days spoken to us by His Son.
- James 1:1: To the twelve tribes which are scattered abroad: Greetings.
- 1 Pet. 1:1: I am writing to God's chosen people.
- 2 Pet. 1:1: I am writing to you who share the same precious faith we have.
- 1 John 1:3: We proclaim to you what we ourselves have actually seen and heard so that you may have fellowship with us.
- 2 John 1:1: The elder unto the elect lady and her children, whom I love in the truth; and not I only, but also all they that have known the truth.
- 3 John 1:1: The elder unto the well-beloved Gaius, whom I love in the truth.
- Jude 1:1: To them that are sanctified by God the Father, and preserved in Jesus Christ, and called.

- Rev. 1:1: To show unto his servants things which must shortly come to pass; and he sent and signified it by his angel unto his servant John.

If someone has never personally spoken in tongues, they should be careful not to criticize what they have not experienced. Instead, readers are encouraged to approach the promise of the Holy Spirit with humility and faith. Clear instructions for receiving the Holy Spirit are provided in the following chapter.

As Scripture reminds us: *"He (Satan) is a liar, and the father of it"* (John 8:44).

Jesus will never harm those who genuinely seek Him. In fact, people often place trust in strangers or unproven sources, yet hesitate to fully trust the God who created them. He is faithful—and worthy of full trust.

John 3:5 is a mandate; Acts 2:38 is its fulfillment.

Obedience to the Word of God requires laying aside man-made traditions and simply following the truth as written. The command to be born of water and Spirit is not optional—it is essential.

Before His ascension, Jesus declared:

The Fullness of the New Birth

"But ye shall receive power, after that the Holy Ghost is come upon you: and ye shall be witnesses unto me..." — Acts 1:8

This power is not mere willpower. Human strength eventually runs out—but the power of the Holy Spirit sustains, transforms, and empowers believers to live holy and fulfill their calling.

Just as a natural birth includes three defining elements, so does spiritual birth:

1. Repentance represents the moment of conception. 2. Baptism represents the entry into the womb of the church, paralleling the water and blood elements. 3. Receiving the Holy Spirit, evidenced by speaking in tongues, signifies the arrival of spiritual life within us. We become the temple of God once born into His family.

Once this process is complete, the believer becomes the **temple of the Holy Spirit** and a full member of God's family.

"Now if any man have not the Spirit of Christ, he is none of his... But if the Spirit of him that raised up Jesus from the dead dwell in you, he that raised up Christ... shall also quicken your mortal bodies..." — Romans 8:9–11

"Who hath also sealed us, and given the earnest of the Spirit in our hearts." — 2 Corinthians 1:22

"...having also given unto us the earnest of the Spirit." — 2 Corinthians 5:5

"...the whole family in heaven and earth is named." — Ephesians 3:14–15

The Fullness of the New Birth

Receive Power

This information can be utilized to assist during evangelism because it serves as a guide for anyone desiring the baptism of the Holy Spirit. Also, it's a practical resource designed to clarify misconceptions and help usher in the manifested presence of God. Anyone personally seeking to be filled, follow these steps.

Jesus stood and cried, saying, "If any man thirst, let him come unto me and drink. He that believeth on me, as the scripture hath said, out of his belly shall flow rivers of living water."
—John 7:37-38

There is **no silent** manifestation of receiving the Holy Spirit. Every time someone was filled with the Holy Spirit in the book of Acts, they spoke in tongues. This super-natural language is always accompanied by power. Many confuse emotional encounters—such as goosebumps, crying, or a warm sensation—with the infilling of the Holy Spirit. While these experiences may indicate that the presence of God is drawing someone, they are **not the same as receiving** the Holy Spirit. These emotional responses signal that God is working in a person's heart, but the true infilling of the Holy Spirit is **evidenced** by speaking in tongues.

*"They were **all** filled with the Holy Ghost, and began to speak with other **tongues**, as the Spirit gave them utterance."* —Acts 2:4

Three barriers the Devil uses to stop us from being filled with the Holy Spirit are: unbelief, unforgiveness, and failure to repent. God can move once we release offenses, activate even a **mustard seed of faith**, and genuinely ask for His blood to cover our transgressions. The Holy Spirit is a **gift and a promise to every believer** of the gospel. Jesus shows no favoritism—if He has given the Holy Spirit to others, **no one** is excluded. Genuine repentance prepares our heart to be filled with the Holy Spirit, even before water baptism. However, the New Birth of water and Spirit is **still a necessary requirement**, so it's crucial **not to overlook** water baptism, **even if** one experiences speaking in tongues beforehand.

Gently remind the candidate that there is no need to fear this beautiful and powerful blessing. Jesus is lovingly knocking at the door of their heart, ready to enter and fill them with His Spirit.

The Fullness of the New Birth

Encourage them to begin with a sincere prayer of repentance out loud, turning their heart fully toward God and conclude by asking the Lord to baptize them with the Holy Spirit and fire. Assure them that their words don't need to be eloquent or polished; they simply need to be **genuine**. As they speak from the heart, we will come into **agreement in faith**, trusting God to do what He has promised.

"If ye then, being evil, know how to give good gifts unto your children: how much more shall your heavenly Father give the Holy Spirit to them that ask him?" — Luke 11:13

Let them know that they can begin speaking in tongues **immediately** if they truly desire the gift and have faith in Him. But if their faith feels weak or unsure, a strategy that has been used for decades in Pentecostal circles is called **"tarrying."** This is not a work of the flesh, but a method of persistent worship that positions us to receive.

Sometimes our faith is strengthened through **praise**, which leads us into God's presence. Encourage them to lift their voice and **repeatedly say, "Thank You, Jesus"** as an expression of worship. This is not vain repetition—it's a focused declaration that **keeps the mind anchored** and heart open. God inhabits the praises of His people, and consistent worship invites the Spirit to move.

As they continue saying, *"Thank You, Jesus, Thank You, Jesus,"* they may find it increasingly difficult to pronounce the phrase clearly. This is often when the **tongue begins to change**, and the **stammering lips** Isaiah spoke of begin to manifest (Isaiah 28:11). Assure them this is not strange—they will not lose control like an exorcism. They are **yielding**, not being overtaken.

The focus isn't on rebuking the devil or praying against darkness—**the power is in the name of Jesus.** Let them know that the Holy Spirit will not force them to speak, but they must **yield their voice** to the Spirit.

As worship flows from the heart, God will begin to **transition them into another language.** It may begin with simple sounds—much like a baby's first words: *"ba-ba," "ma-ma," "da-da."* That's how many heavenly languages begin. Encourage them **not to rationalize it**—the Spirit flows from the inner man, not the intellect.

If they inwardly hear unfamiliar sounds, tell them to **speak them out boldly**. Just as we prepare our response in a normal conversation, the Spirit will give utterance—**we simply release it by**

The Fullness of the New Birth

faith. We cannot speak two languages at once, so as their tongue "stammers," they must embrace the shift. This is not mere babble from repetition—it is the Holy Spirit **desiring to speak through them.** Encourage the candidate to continue releasing those unfamiliar sounds with confidence.

"But God hath chosen the foolish things of the world to confound the wise..."
— 1 Corinthians 1:27

They may not understand what they are saying, and that's okay. Understanding only comes if God gives the interpretation. As they yield, the language will become more fluent and pronounced. Remind them: **the enemy will try to plant doubt**, making them think it's made up or fake—but this is the Holy Spirit working through them.

Encourage them to **open and close their mouth** as they would in a regular conversation. This physical cooperation with the Spirit helps release the flow of tongues.

"For he that speaketh in an unknown tongue speaketh not unto men, but unto God: for no man understandeth him; howbeit in the spirit he speaketh mysteries." — 1 Corinthians 14:2

Reassure them that **Jesus deeply loves them** and longs for them to be empowered. They don't have to worry about saying anything wrong. Help them relax and **let the Holy Spirit flow**, using all the faculties of speech, much like learning vowels (A, E, I, O, U).

They are not giving themselves the Holy Ghost—**He is speaking through them** as God gives the utterance.

Praying in tongues allows us to **speak directly to God** from our spirit. It is a personal and powerful prayer language that edifies the believer and aligns us with God's perfect will.

Encouraging someone to praise God in anticipation of the outpouring—and to yield to the stammer as a sign of transition—often leads to powerful results. This method has been proven for decades in Pentecostalism.

The Fullness of the New Birth

Deliverance

Society has normalized sinful lifestyles, but embracing that mindset leads to spiritual mediocrity. The enemy thrives in deception, often lulling people into a state of complacency. Yet, the Word of God is filled with accounts of deliverance and healing—but in each case, **faith and action** were required. If you're seeking freedom, it's time to put your faith into motion. Your internal battles can and will be **annihilated** as you remain steadfast in the Lord. There is **power and total deliverance** in the name of **Jesus Christ!**

Deliverance doesn't always happen overnight. While God certainly has the power to bring **instant freedom**, many of us walk through a **process of transformation** as we grow in Christ. Don't condemn yourself for past or present mistakes—**salvation is the beginning of a lifelong journey.** Breaking free from sinful habits takes intentional effort and a daily decision to live righteously.

Practical Wisdom for the Journey:

Don't dwell on the past—it leads to depression.

Don't worry about the future—it leads to anxiety.

Take one day at a time.

As a **new creature in Christ**, give yourself grace. **Avoid comparing** your journey to others who may have been walking this path longer. Sometimes, **we are our own greatest enemy**. You must make a **sober decision** to save yourself from yourself. The flesh has brought us to many dead ends, but only what we do **for Christ will last.**

Your decision to turn your back on sin is a **courageous** one. Don't forget—**we all start somewhere**. Even if the process feels scary, **do it afraid**. We live in a world where sin is ever-present, but be intentional about what you allow into your spirit. Watching sexualized content, listening to profane or explicit music, and keeping company with those who gossip or curse excessively will **contaminate your spirit** and hinder your purification process.

Be Strategic: Identify what influences you negatively. Pinpoint the hindrances that weaken your walk. Awareness leads to deliverance.

The Fullness of the New Birth

Holiness is not accidental—it's a daily, deliberate decision.

In a spiritual context, **strongholds** are deeply rooted beliefs, mindsets, or habits that resist the truth of God's Word. These may appear as **addictions, fears, deceptions**, or even toxic thought patterns that keep you in bondage. Walking through deliverance may feel painful, but the **power of the Holy Spirit** surrounds you with God's love and draws you toward purpose.

There are **levels in the spirit realm**, and **obedience** is what ushers us into spiritual maturity. Instead of fixating on your struggles, begin to **fill every void with worship and prayer**. If you truly desire transformation, **God will do it.**

"Behold, I am the Lord, the God of all flesh: is there anything too hard for me?"
— Jeremiah 32:27

The Word of God is a **cleansing agent**. It purifies the mind and conditions the heart.

"For the word of God is quick, and powerful, and sharper than any twoedged sword..." — Hebrews 4:12

As you read the Scriptures, the Holy Spirit begins to **work inwardly**, exposing fleshly attitudes and reshaping your inner life. Don't hide behind excuses like, *"That's just who I am."*

True transformation doesn't come through stubbornness—it comes through **surrender**.

As believers read the Word of God, they must also **apply it to their daily lives** (James 1:22–24). God blesses **submission**, and through that obedience, transformation occurs. Christians operate by a **standard of holiness** as they are continually renewed in Christ. Jesus declared, *"It is written: 'Man shall not live on bread alone, but on every word that comes from the mouth of God'"* (Matthew 4:4, NIV).

Being discipled under a **Bible-based, Spirit-filled church** is essential. It is spiritually dangerous to live as a wandering sheep, disconnected from a shepherd. Every believer should remain under **Pastoral covering** and remain accountable to leadership. The adversary thrives on **isolation**, drawing people away from safety and into vulnerability.

Even seemingly **minor decisions** should be taken to God in prayer. A small misstep can result in larger consequences over time. It is prideful to believe one has all the answers. Scripture affirms, *"In the multitude of counselors there is safety"* (Proverbs 11:14). Seeking

The Fullness of the New Birth

counsel from **spiritually mature believers** provides clarity and protection.

If the Lord sends an **accountability partner**, it is important not to reject help out of familiarity with struggle. Some become so used to wrestling in silence that they resist the very assistance sent to free them. The enemy operates through **darkness and shame**, but transparency and spiritual support bring healing. A trusted confidant can help prevent the buildup of frustration and break through spiritual stagnation.

Perfection is not possible in this life. *"If we say that we have no sin, we deceive ourselves, and the truth is not in us"* (1 John 1:8). However, as a believer **surrenders their will to God**, their desires begin to reflect His nature and character. Deliverance becomes more evident as the person grows in spiritual maturity.

"Run from anything that stimulates youthful lusts. Instead, pursue righteous living, faithfulness, love, and peace. Enjoy the companionship of those who call on the Lord with pure hearts."
—2 Timothy 2:22 (NLT)

Emotional healing is also critical for spiritual progress. Letting go of **grudges** and **past trauma** opens the mind to envision a brighter future. Forgiveness is more than an emotion—it is an **act of the will** that pardons offenses and extends grace, even to enemies. It is not optional; it is a **requirement for deliverance.**

Deliverance comes to the **desperate**, and healing to the **humble**. As taught in 1 Corinthians 13:4–5, **unselfish love** is foundational to forgiveness, for love *"keeps no record of wrongs."* More importantly, forgiving others is **directly connected** to receiving God's forgiveness:

"If you forgive those who sin against you, your heavenly Father will forgive you. But if you refuse to forgive others, your Father will not forgive your sins." —Matthew 6:14–15 (NLT)

Deliverance often occurs in stages—**30, 60, and 100-fold** (Mark 4:20). A new believer in the **30-fold stage** may still battle with certain sinful habits while genuinely striving to live right. These struggles should not be mistaken for failure or lost salvation. Staying faithful under pressure allows God to **build strength and character**.

As maturity increases, the believer enters the **60-fold stage**. At this level, they gain **self-control** and learn to **resist temptation** more consistently. This is a significant milestone in the spiritual journey. The foundation of their relationship with Christ becomes firmer, and they

The Fullness of the New Birth

experience **fellowship with other believers**. While trials will still come, the believer now walks with a deeper awareness that **God is present through every battle**.

The evidence of **100-fold deliverance** is when a believer no longer practices the sins that once enslaved them. In this stage, the enemy is forced to **devise new strategies** because the believer has matured beyond old pitfalls and habits.

Here, **perfection** doesn't mean flawlessness—it means **spiritual maturity**. The believer's goal is twofold:

To reach a place of transformation where the **past no longer defines them**, and to walk in **contentment**, fully embracing who they are and where God has positioned them.

"And do not be conformed to this world: but be ye transformed by the renewing of your mind, that ye may prove what is that good (30), and acceptable (60), and perfect (100) will of God."
— Romans 12:2

To reach this stage, the mind must be transformed—this includes one's thought patterns, emotional responses, and overall presentation. **Discipline is vital.** In the 100-fold dimension of deliverance, there is **no inner desire to return to the past**. The believer is fully committed to living in God's **perfect will**, with a heart no longer seeking to please the flesh but to **please the Father.**

This kind of transformation is possible for anyone. As one who testifies to being **fully delivered after 20 years of living as a transgender male**—proof that God can liberate anyone from any lifestyle or identity that is outside His will. The journey may not be without its challenges, but stumbling is not the same as failing. **Baptism in the name of Jesus Christ** remains a necessity; it washes away past sins, and the blood of Jesus covers every future mistake when genuine repentance is present.

The Battle of the Mind

Spiritual warfare at this stage intensifies. The enemy primarily attacks the **mind**—bringing up old memories, temptations, or visual triggers in an attempt to lure the believer back into bondage. If Satan can't get someone to dwell on the past, he may instead assign people to distract or discourage their growth.

Be alert. Stay focused. Remain determined.

As one preacher wisely said, *"Before you decide to give up, remember—this time next year, you'll be grateful you kept going."*

The Fullness of the New Birth

The 100-fold stage is not about perfection in performance—it's about **maturity in identity**. The believer knows who they are, whom they serve, and why they can't go back. True deliverance redefines how one sees life, purpose, and power. And that level of transformation can only come by **abiding in Christ and walking in the Spirit** daily.

"If the Son therefore shall make you free, ye shall be free indeed." — John 8:36

Stand Firm and Don't Go Back

Breakdown of Galatians 5:1 in the Context of Deliverance: "Stand fast" means to hold your ground, remain firm, and refuse to waver.

The **liberty** Christ gives refers to **freedom from sin, legalism, condemnation, and spiritual bondage**. It is deliverance from anything that once had power over you—whether addiction, demonic influence, toxic thought patterns, or religious deception.

This liberty is **not self-earned**. It is a **gift from Jesus through the cross**, and it must be **actively guarded**. Freedom can be lost if it is not preserved through intentional living and spiritual awareness.

"...and be not entangled again with the yoke of bondage."

The "**yoke of bondage**" symbolizes anything that enslaves you—whether it be sin, empty religious rituals, or past strongholds.

"**Entangled again**" suggests a return to the very things God already delivered you from. This often happens when believers **neglect intimacy with God**, becoming vulnerable to old behaviors, thought cycles, and unhealthy connections.

Paul's warning is urgent: **Don't go back.** Deliverance is not just a **moment**—it is a **lifestyle**. Freedom requires **daily maintenance**.

Religious performance is not liberty. True freedom flows from relationship, not ritual.

Backsliding becomes a real threat when believers forget what they've been delivered from.

This verse is a charge to **stay free—spiritually, emotionally, and mentally**.

Christ didn't set you free to live in cycles. Stand firm, stay rooted, and don't look back.

Practical Advice for Protecting Your Deliverance

The Fullness of the New Birth

Do not let the Devil convince you that taking precautions is too extreme.

Sometimes, **spiritual boundaries are practical steps**. If changing your phone number helps you avoid temptation—**do it**. If moving, disconnecting, or cutting off unhealthy ties is necessary—**obey**. Deliverance must be **defended**.

As a **new creature in Christ**, you are called to create **new memories** that glorify God.

Sin is not a necessity—it is a choice.

The opposite of **temptation** is **contentment** in Christ.

Be mindful of **interactions with unsaved friends**. These connections, while seemingly harmless, can become entrapment's. They may remind you of the past or create false nostalgia. You must remain **prayerful and discerning** in such relationships.

If the **Holy Spirit urges you to disconnect**, don't ignore it—even if it's sentimental. Some people are afraid of your transformation because they fear **losing their bond with you**. Remember: you are no longer the same person. **Do not seek validation from those who want to keep you in your past.**

In **2002**, after initially giving my life to Christ, I fell back into the world just **nine months later**. Entertaining updates from my past deceived me into believing I was **missing out**. That deception cost me **12 more years** of fellowship with God until I fully returned in **2014**.

The enemy's goal is always to **lure you back into sin**. Even well-meaning people can become distractions if they're not walking in the Spirit. Stay sharp. Stay prayerful. **Do not be deceived—stay focused on your walk with God.**

"Bad company corrupts good character."
—1 Corinthians 15:33 (NLT)

Cutting ties with **former lovers or past sexual partners** is **essential for true deliverance**. Remaining emotionally or socially connected to them creates **soulish bonds** that can keep **lust active within the emotions**. What may begin as innocent communication can easily evolve into **casual sexual encounters** because of past familiarity and spiritual residue.

Believers must **not assume** that someone's salvation depends solely on their personal evangelism. If the Holy Spirit is truly drawing that individual, **God can use anyone**—He has millions of laborers in His vineyard. Staying

The Fullness of the New Birth

connected out of obligation can trap a person in a **vicious emotional and spiritual cycle**.

A crucial question must be asked:
How can one be who they were and who they are—at the same time?
The answer is—we cannot.

It is **dangerous** to surround oneself with the **very spirits** they are trying to be delivered from.

> A sheep cries when it falls into the mud. A pig **willingly wallows** in it.

The **prodigal son** (Luke 15:11–32) didn't find restoration until he recognized he was **living beneath his privilege**. Feeding pigs and desiring their food became his wake-up call. Similarly, believers must realize that **following Christ** offers not only **spiritual life** but also **natural and emotional restoration—if** they are willing to leave the past behind.

"Let us strip off every weight that slows us down, especially the sin that so easily trips us up. And let us run with endurance the race God has set before us." — Hebrews 12:1 (NLT)

"Greater is HE that is in me than he that is in the world." — 1 John 4:4

The Power of Renunciation in Deliverance

Renunciation is a declaration of refusal—a firm decision to no longer follow, obey, or support something. Spiritually speaking, to **renounce** is to **relinquish the enemy's legal access** and serve him an **eviction notice**.

"Death and life are in the power of the tongue." — Proverbs 18:21

This verse reminds us that **our words carry authority**. That's why **renunciations should be spoken aloud**, not read silently. **Victory produces a sound.** In deliverance, the believer's voice becomes a **weapon** against the forces of darkness.

When spoken with **boldness and fervency**, renunciations:

1. Break soul ties
2. Close spiritual doors
3. Release angelic assistance
4. Reinforce the believer's alignment with the will of God

Renunciations are not mere words—they are acts of spiritual warfare. They send a clear message to the enemy that **his access has been revoked**, and his assignment is canceled.

Say aloud:
"I renounce all **soul ties** in the name of Jesus. I

The Fullness of the New Birth

renounce every **spirit of lust** that is interlocked with the occult in the name of Jesus. I renounce **perversion**, including role-playing, lesbianism, fornication, pornography, adultery, masturbation, and fantasy, in the name of Jesus.

I renounce and command all **spirits of impurity, lust, and perversion** to leave my **mind, will, and emotions** in the name of Jesus. I break all **curses of molestation, rape, incest, promiscuity, perversion** and **addiction** in the mighty name of Jesus. I renounce and cast out thoughts of **shame, condemnation, unworthiness, and guilt** in the name of Jesus.

I renounce all **strongholds of alcohol, drugs, and any illegal substances** in the name of Jesus. I command all **spirits that make me feel lonely and desperate for a companion** to flee now in the name of Jesus. I command all **spirits of incubus and succubus** to leave my body, including my sexual organs, in the name of Jesus. *(Incubus and succubus are sexual night demons that arouse individuals in their sleep.)*

I renounce all **spirits of hurt, rejection, depression, neglect, anger, retaliation, fear, grief, bitterness, unforgiveness, anxiety, confusion, and hopelessness**—loose my **will, emotions, and mind** in the name of Jesus! I renounce and command any **addictive**

personality I have inherited to leave my **appetite** in the name of Jesus. I renounce all **generational spirits of rebellion** in my bloodline in the name of Jesus.

I renounce all **spirits of narcissism, arrogance, ego, stubbornness, pride, disobedience, self-will, and self-deception** in the name of Jesus. I forgive **anyone who has offended, abused, distressed, rejected, or abandoned me**, in the name of Jesus. I command **any spirit that I am unaware of** but is active in my life to leave now in the name of Jesus. As I grow closer to the Lord, my **desires will evolve. Freedom is my portion in the name of Jesus Christ! Amen.**

The Lord wants you to experience genuine joy. I speak over your life total deliverance in the mighty name of JESUS CHRIST! You will not go back to a lifestyle of habitual sin. The Holy Ghost will guide you into a pathway of righteousness. The glory of the future is the joy of the present. Whatever you have to give up is going to be worth it! Be content in Christ and live for HIM!!

We must be consistent with our attendance at church. The Devil attempts to use self-doubt to make one feel inadequate. Some awkwardness may occur, but we must reject the idea that we do not fit the criteria of other men/women in the

The Fullness of the New Birth

congregation. The House of God is for **everyone** and the blood of Jesus was shed for all of humanity.

The Lord knows how to bless us with spiritual friends. Our life has already been planned from start to finish. God is in divine control and has promised to be alongside us every step of the way. We can make this journey!

We cannot please God if we do not believe that He is able to do what **seems impossible**. The battlefield of the mind is real, but choosing to focus on uplifting and optimistic thoughts weakens negativity's grip and creates space for true joy. Some chatter is not even worth addressing—it is simply an attack to distract.

Faith is trusting God even when the outcome isn't yet visible. He promises to bring liberation through prayer and fasting. If you've never fasted before, start gradually. During the times you would normally eat, devote that time to prayer, worship, and reading the Word.

Fasting isn't about starving yourself or barely eating until deliverance transpires. It's about disciplining the flesh and drawing closer to God. A helpful approach is to fast consistently—perhaps two days a week during specific hours—for a set period of time. Maintain a consistent fasting regimen for as long as it takes to receive your breakthrough.

Fasting, prayer, and immersing ourselves in God's Word are the most important tools for deliverance. Empowerment flows when you engage in spiritual disciplines. Sacrificing food to seek God grabs His attention. He will set you free from the burden of others' opinions, helping you understand that **comparison** is a fast track to misery. On your fasting days, drink only water during those hours. If health conditions or medications prevent you from going without food, consider refraining from other activities you enjoy, such as coffee, candy, social media, unnecessary phone conversations, television, or other comforts unrelated to food.

Fasting tears down the wall of the flesh and helps you maintain a healthy attitude.

"And he (Jesus) said unto them, this kind can come forth by nothing, but by prayer and fasting."
—Mark 9:29

If you are single, your sexual desires may intensify as you begin to starve them. The spirit of lust and perversion will tempt you with suggestions to satisfy your flesh. However, bondage loses its strength through fasting. Prayer and fasting awaken the Spirit of God

The Fullness of the New Birth

within you, purging strongholds with a refining fire. You cannot receive the promises of God with a carnal mindset. A desire for holiness will grow, benefiting your spiritual walk.

"Is not this the fast that I have chosen? to loose the bands of wickedness, to undo the heavy burdens, and to let the oppressed go free, and that ye break every yoke?" —Isaiah 58:6

"And he (Jesus) said unto them, this kind can come forth by nothing, but by prayer and fasting." —Mark 9:29

Our 21st-century culture can lead us to becoming numb to what matters to the Lord. Jesus did not waver as to whether His church would fast. He said, "When you fast," — not "if" (Matthew 6:16-17). As you detox the spirit and become consumed with desire and praise for God, you become sensitive to His voice.

When you acknowledge through fasting that you need God to live, and to live more abundantly, you will begin to desire God in a new way. Realizing you need God more than food will make you appreciate what the Psalmist meant when he wrote, "Like the deer that pants after water, my soul longs for You" (Psalm 42:1). His purpose and plan are totally different from your will and your way.

Pace yourself, and if you have to concentrate on one thing at a time, that is perfectly fine. Whatever reminds you of the past in a negative sense or serves as a portal of temptation, get rid of it. The will of God is accomplished through obedience. If the Holy Spirit leads you to discard things, know that you will receive blessings in a greater magnitude. Alcohol, street drugs, porn sites, sex toys, Ouija boards, tarot cards, energy crystals, sage, chakra, mobile apps used for casual sexual hookups, and explicit photos are examples of things that should be eliminated. Unusual distress is caused from significant life changes while detaching from people, places, or articles.

Prayer has power over everything. Our communication with God strengthens day by day. Prayer is not always about asking God for something. We cannot pray selfishly and expect godly results. Sometimes it's an expression of feelings released toward the Lord, as if we are speaking directly to a friend in front of us. Exercising faith produces a confident prayer life in which we believe that God hears our prayers and will answer them. God is an invisible being. It may seem like He is far away, but His Word declares that He will never leave or forsake us (Hebrews 13:5). Sometimes we just need to thank Him while praying and worship Him for who

The Fullness of the New Birth

He is. Worship removes the struggle of toiling with demonic forces.

A strong prayer life imparts inner strength, wisdom, understanding, guidance, spiritual gifts, joy, peace, and freedom from fear. Our ability to change a situation is often shaped by how we perceive ourselves. When our passion for God fills our heart, it is reflected in our prayers. Acknowledging blessings we did not earn cultivates gratitude.

"The effectual fervent prayer of a righteous man availeth much." —James 5:16

Our spirit is strengthened as our relationship with God deepens. Transformation begins internally, aligning our heart and mind with His will. As we grow in Christ, He may also refine our outward appearance, especially if it once reflected a culture **contrary** to godliness. The beauty of walking with Christ is that He gradually removes old habits and reshapes us in His image. When the inward transformation is complete, it will be evident outwardly. This does NOT mean we cannot be fashionable.

I realize that people can take legalism too far. In 1 Samuel 16:7, God sought a faithful heart when He said, *"This is the one,"* in choosing David (1 Samuel 16:12). Some misuse this passage to suggest that appearance as a child of God is unimportant. While outward looks can be deceiving, a true conversion in Christ leads to a life of **order and decency**. If appearance were insignificant, I could have remained a transgender male. *"If any man be in Christ, he is a new creature"* (2 Corinthians 5:17). How we present ourselves is a reflection of our hearts.

This guidance is not meant to create anxiety but to awaken awareness of habits that may have gone unnoticed. Walking in God's divine purpose brings favor, and obedience leads to abundant blessings. Jesus walks with us every step of the way. Do not be overwhelmed by rules—rather, embrace the process of being molded by the Potter's hands (Jeremiah 18:1-10). Take these insights as constructive tools for your complete deliverance. God will not lead us astray.

Now, let's explore the vital role sanctification plays in our spiritual growth. To sanctify means to be set apart. God calls us to live free from condemnation, no longer enslaved by the enemy. Sanctification does not stop after obeying Acts 2:38—it is an **ongoing journey**, and through it, we are continually blessed.

The battle is between our old sinful nature and the new life led by the Spirit. While the heart desires to obey God, the flesh is weak, making

The Fullness of the New Birth

sin a constant struggle. Yet, it is in this ongoing battle that sanctification takes root, refining us and strengthening our obedience to God.

"For the flesh lusts against the Spirit, and the Spirit against the flesh; and these are contrary to one another, so that you do not do the things that you wish." —Galatians 5:17 (NKJV)

Sanctification is an inward spiritual process in which God, through the Holy Spirit, purifies and transforms us. We all encounter struggles that hinder us from living the life God desires. As we grow, the Holy Spirit convicts us of areas that need correction, guiding us into a lifestyle of holiness. We become more aware of our actions, surroundings, and associations through a biblical lens. Our purpose is not tied to comfort but to the will of God.

During this training ground, you may experience loneliness. However, God is omnipresent—He is always with you. This season of isolation is a time of strengthening, preparing you for a lifelong commitment to Christ. You are His masterpiece, and He is proud of your growth. When you feel forgotten, remember that you are not—God has assigned an angel to watch over you. Seeking therapy alongside your spiritual renewal can also help you **heal** from past wounds.

Praying in tongues edifies your spirit, aligns you with God's will, and empowers you to overcome the desires of the flesh. It is the highest form of agreement in prayer, bringing relief from worry and stress. When you engage in your heavenly language, the Holy Spirit performs deep emotional healing, mending past disappointments and failures. There were times I lay beside my bed, praying in tongues so long that I fell asleep in the presence of the Lord.

Your spiritual survival depends on prayer and applying God's Word. Do not put yourself in situations that invite temptation. Proverbs 6:27 warns against *"taking fire into your bosom,"* meaning we should avoid compromising positions that can lead to sin. If you stumble, do not justify staying in sin. *"If you confess your sins, He is faithful and just to forgive you and cleanse you from all unrighteousness"* (1 John 1:9).

Build a relationship with God that keeps you from sin—not out of fear, but because of your deep love for Him.

Please do not feel discouraged or defeated if you have followed these steps yet still struggle with temptation. Overcoming past sins takes time, and everyone's journey in the Spirit progresses differently. Struggling with a stronghold will not send you to hell, but practicing sin or endorsing

The Fullness of the New Birth

those who indulge in it (Ephesians 5:7) leads to spiritual destruction (Revelation 21:7-8).

Through consistency and discipline in your spiritual walk, the layers of bondage will be peeled away like an onion. God is able! Even if you still face challenges, as long as your progressive efforts are evident, do not hesitate to testify of God's goodness. Satan wants to muzzle you. Decree The word of God to yield its fruit of manifestation.

"Behold, I am the LORD, the God of all flesh: is there anything too hard for me?"
—Jeremiah 32:27

Remember, we must fight for your freedom—deliverance must be pursued with intentionality. Some become content with a 30 or 60-fold progression, making excuses for their internal struggles, but this does not have to be your permanent state. Even if you don't immediately experience a change in feelings or the eradication of sinful habits, do not accept those struggles as your identity.

We must allow the Holy Spirit to rule over your flesh. Feed on the Word of God and let it take root in our spirit. Exercise faith and believe that your full 100-fold manifestation is on the way! Keep attending church, it's a lifeline for discipleship. I guarantee you that as you remain steadfast and make sound decisions, those behaviors will cease. The only way you can fail is if you give up—no matter what, you must remain faithful.

Jesus healed many instantly, while others improved as they went. Full deliverance is available to everyone because God does not show favoritism (Acts 10:34). What He has done for one, He will do for another. I can only speak from experience—these steps worked for me. Through abiding in the secret place of prayer and fasting, I was purged inwardly from unnatural desires, lust, addictions, and more.

"And from the days of John the Baptist until now the kingdom of heaven suffereth violence, and the violent take it by force." —Matthew 11:12

An article in the *Full Life Study Bible* expounds on this verse, explaining: "The kingdom of heaven is taken hold of only by forceful people who are committed to breaking away from sinful and immoral lifestyles. No matter what the cost, such people vigorously seek the kingdom in all its power. Turning to Christ, His Word, and His righteous ways are the pathway to peace. In other words, experiencing the kingdom of heaven and all its blessings requires earnest endeavor.

The Fullness of the New Birth

This is a fight of faith, accompanied by a strong will to resist Satan, sin, and a perverse society."

We will not be successful in our walk with the Lord if we rarely pray, compromise with the world, neglect the Word of God, and lack spiritual hunger. We must stay diligent, stay hungry, and fight for your transformation! The spirit of holiness has been imparted and is outwardly visible. You are content with your new identity and embracing it joyfully.

"I will give thanks to You, for I am fearfully and wonderfully made; Wonderful are Your works, and my soul knows it very well."
—Psalm 139:14 NASB

Continue to take one day at a time. Do not slack up on your prayer life. Commit to a day of fasting at least every other week. Stay in fellowship with mature Christians to keep you accountable. He that has begun a good work will perform it until the day of Jesus Christ. Let your light shine that men may see your good works and glorify our Father in heaven. Godliness with contentment is great gain (Phil. 1:6, Matt. 5:18, 1 Tim. 6:6).

Whatever is valuable should be protected.

Keep a balanced life, and make sure that what you think is discernment is not fear or paranoia either. God has great things in store! Keep shining on the winning team for Jesus! Remember this, the enemy is going to test your deliverance, but as you remain in prayer and studying the Word of God your strength to resist temptation will lift up a standard.

As we grow in Christ, we become more effective soul winners and living examples of holiness. Even our struggles can inspire others as they witness our perseverance. I pray this book has served as a tool of empowerment and encouragement on your journey.

Fly High as God exceeds your expectations!

The Fullness of the New Birth

Benefits of the Holy Spirit

Helps Us- Rom. 8:26
Guides Us- Jn. 16:13
Teaches Us- Jn. 14:26
Speaks- Rev. 2:7
Reveals- 1 Cor. 2:10
Instructs- Acts 8:29
Testifies of Jesus- Jn. 15:26
Comforts Us -Acts 9:31
Calls Us -Acts 13:2
Fills Us -Acts 4:31
He Strengthens Us- Eph. 3:16
Prays for Us- Rom. 8:26
Prophesies Through Us- 2 Pet. 1:21
Bears Witness to the Truth- Rom. 9:1
Brings Joy- 1 Thess. 1:6
Brings Freedom- 2 Cor. 3:17
Helps to Obey- 1 Pet. 1:22
Calls for Jesus' Return- Rev. 22:17
Transforms Us- 2 Cor. 3:18
Lives in Us- 1 Cor. 3:16
Frees Us- Rom. 8:2
Renews Us- Titus 3:5
Gives Gifts- 1 Cor. 12:8-10
Produces Fruit in Us- Gal. 5:22-23
Leads Us- Rom. 8:14
Convicts- Jn. 16:8
Sanctifies Us- 2 Thess. 2:13

Empowers Us- Acts 1:8
Unites Us- Eph. 4:3-4
Seals Us- Eph. 1:13
Gives Access to the Father- Eph. 2:18
Enables Us to Wait- Gal. 5:5
Casts Out Demons- Matt. 12:28

www.ingramcontent.com/pod-product-compliance
Lightning Source LLC
LaVergne TN
LVHW091318080426
835510LV00007B/536